NOBODY PARTICULAR

Printed in Canada on recycled paper.
First printing, August 2005
10 9 8 7 6 5 4 3 2 1

Recycled Paper
Chelsea Green sees publishing as a tool for cultural change and ecological stewardship. We strive
to align our book manufacturing practices with our editorial mission, and to reduce the impact
of our business enterprise on the environment. We print our books and catalogs on chlorine-free
recycled paper, using soy-based inks, whenever possible. Chelsea Green is a member of the Green
Press Initiative (www.greenpressinitiative.org), a nonprofit coalition of publishers, manufacturers,
and authors working to protect the world's endangered forests and conserve natural resources.
   Nobody Particular was printed on New Life Recycled Smooth Opaque White, a 30 percent
post-consumer waste recycled, old growth forest-free paper supplied by Marquis.

Library of Congress Cataloging-in-Publication Data
Bang, Molly.
Nobody particular / by Molly Bang
1. Chemical plants—Waste disposal—Environmental aspects—Texas—Juvenile literature. 2. Environmental
protection—Texas—Citizen participation—Juvenile literature. 3. Environmentalism—Texas—Juvenile literature.
[1. Water—Pollution. 2. Pollution. 3. Environmental protection—Citizen participation.] II. Title.
TD195.C45B35   2000   363.738'4-dc21
ISBN 1-931498-94-6

The color borders in this book were done in gouache; the black-and-white interior illustrations were a mix
of photographs taken in Texas and drawings in India ink and white paint, with some patterned overlays.
The newspaper clipping on page 7 is courtesy of the *Victoria Advocate*.
The photographs on pages 40 and 43 are courtesy of the U.S. Coast Guard.

Chelsea Green Publishing Company
P.O. Box 428
White River Junction, VT 05001
800-639-4099
www.chelseagreen.com

Bay water is a mix of salty seawater and freshwater from rivers and streams.
Many creatures need to live in the bays for part of their lives.

NOBODY PARTICULAR

ONE WOMAN'S FIGHT TO SAVE THE BAYS

THE DIANE WILSON STORY

MOLLY BANG

CHELSEA GREEN PUBLISHING COMPANY

WHITE RIVER JUNCTION, VERMONT

I give thanks for clean water. —M. B.

This book began when I told Margaret Morgan-Hubbard that I wanted to make books about people who make a difference. Margaret said, "You should meet Diane Wilson." Thank you, Margaret, and also many, many thanks to Conner Bailey, Jim Blackburn, Ivette Candela, Penny Chisholm, Jason Clay, Gregg Eckhardt, Johnny French, J. Brent Giezentanner, David Gray, Jim Green, Phil Gschwend, Keelung Hong, Ruth Hubbard, Joan Lederman, Mangrove Action Network, Jack Matson, Robert McFarlane, Ken Mounger, Carol Reinisch, *Rachel's Health and Environmental Weekly*, *Texas Shores*, Carol Verburg, and of course thanks, love, and joy to Diane Wilson.

Shrimp hatch from eggs in the salty Gulf water, then move to the sweeter bays and river mouths to grow into adults. In a year, they return to the Gulf to spawn and die.

THIS STORY I'M ABOUT TO TELL YOU IS TRUE, NEAR AS I CAN MAKE IT. IT'S MY OWN STORY. MY NAME IS DIANE WILSON. I'M A SHRIMPER OUT OF SEADRIFT, IN CALHOUN COUNTY, TEXAS.

MY DADDY, GRANPA, AND GREAT-GRANPA FISHED THESE EAST TEXAS BAYS. MY HUSBAND AND BROTHERS ARE SHRIMPERS, TOO, SCRATCHING FOR A LIVING. HARD LABOR. EVERYTHING'S ALWAYS BREAKING. BANK OWNS YOU. AND THIS YEAR'S BEEN MISERABLE.

NOTHIN'!

FISH FOR LEGAL-SIZED SHRIMP AND GET NOTHIN'.

FISH UP BIG HAULS OF BABIES . . .

. . . AND THAT'S OUR WHOLE FUTURE SQUIRMIN' AND DYIN' ON THE DECK.

BUT THESE WATERS ARE MY WHOLE LIFE. I AM THESE BAYS. SO BEING A SHRIMPER—

IT'S KIND OF LIKE BEING CURSED WITH A HOLY ADDICTION, I GUARANTEE YOU.

YOU'RE A STRANGE BIRD, DIANE WILSON.

YOU'RE THE ONLY WOMAN OUT THERE SHRIMPIN' ALONE...

BUT YOU'RE ALWAYS READIN' AND READIN'...

YOU WERE HEAD OF THE PTA WITH YOUR BABIES IN SCHOOL...

...SO HOW COME YOU'RE DOIN' A MAN'S WORK ON THE BAY? YOU OUGHTA TEACH SCHOOL LIKE YOUR SISTERS.

YOU GOT NOTHIN', DIANE.

WORSE, I GOT LEGAL-SIZED SHRIMP, BUT THEY'RE BABIES.

MY DADDY'D BE ASHAMED.

DON'T WE KNOW WHAT WE'RE DOIN' TO OURSELVES?

WE GOTTA LET THESE SHRIMP GROW INTO ADULTS— 'SPECIALLY IN THESE LEAN YEARS —OR PRETTY SOON WE'LL ONLY HAVE FARMED SHRIMP AND IMPORTS!

BUT WE GOTTA EAT NOW! WHAT ELSE CAN WE DO?

WHAT I CAN DO IS PICK UP THREE OF THE KIDS, BUY SOME BEANS, CORNMEAL....

BUT ON JUNE 20, 1989, THIS NORMAL, EVERYDAY LIFE OF MINE CHANGES IN A FLASH.

Shrimp eat mostly single-celled animals and plants, as well as plant and animal detritus. Many, MANY animals eat shrimp.

A FRIEND HANDS ME THE DAY'S PAPER, WHICH TALKS ABOUT A REPORT ON POLLUTION.

IT'S A GOVERNMENT REPORT,

HEY, DIANE! LOOK AT THIS!

SAYING THAT LAST YEAR THE CHEMICAL PLANTS IN TEXAS GAVE OUT THE MOST POLLUTION OF ANY STATE IN THE U.S.!

BET YOU THOUGHT OUR LI'L OL' CALHOUN COUNTY WAS FAMOUS 'CAUSE WE'RE POOR!

TURNS OUT WE'RE AT THE TOP OF THE HEAP!

THEN I SEE WHAT MY FRIEND'S TALKING ABOUT.

Texas also accounted for one third of the total toxic discharges onto the land, with 835 million pounds. Calhoun County ranked first nationally accounting for 54 percent of the state's total, followed by Milam

HOW MUCH OF THAT TOXIC DISCHARGE FLOWS RIGHT INTO THIS WATER? WE MAY BE POOR, BUT THIS IS JUST WRONG. I'M GOING TO STOP IT. I'M GOING TO PROTECT THESE BAYS.

Shrimp are one tiny part of the bay ecosystem.
Before human disturbance, bays were
nearly as diverse as coral reefs and rain
forests, and even more productive.

GUADALUPE RIVER

SAN ANTONIO BAY

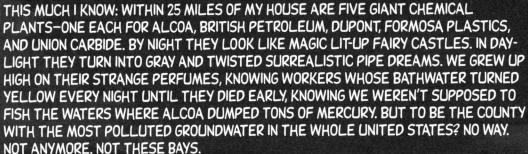

THIS MUCH I KNOW: WITHIN 25 MILES OF MY HOUSE ARE FIVE GIANT CHEMICAL PLANTS—ONE EACH FOR ALCOA, BRITISH PETROLEUM, DUPONT, FORMOSA PLASTICS, AND UNION CARBIDE. BY NIGHT THEY LOOK LIKE MAGIC LIT-UP FAIRY CASTLES. IN DAY-LIGHT THEY TURN INTO GRAY AND TWISTED SURREALISTIC PIPE DREAMS. WE GREW UP HIGH ON THEIR STRANGE PERFUMES, KNOWING WORKERS WHOSE BATHWATER TURNED YELLOW EVERY NIGHT UNTIL THEY DIED EARLY, KNOWING WE WEREN'T SUPPOSED TO FISH THE WATERS WHERE ALCOA DUMPED TONS OF MERCURY. BUT TO BE THE COUNTY WITH THE MOST POLLUTED GROUNDWATER IN THE WHOLE UNITED STATES? NO WAY. NOT ANYMORE. NOT THESE BAYS.

NOW, I'M NOBODY PARTICULAR—JUST A SHRIMPER AND MOMMA—NO EDUCATION, NO MONEY, NO CLOUT. HOW CAN A NOBODY MAKE THESE CORPORATIONS QUIT DUMPING THEIR POISONS ON US? IF I STOP TO THINK ON IT, I'LL KNOW I'M A FOOL AND GO PATCH A SHRIMP NET, QUIET MY MIND IN MOVING TWINE AND FINGERS.

SO BEFORE I CAN THINK, I CALL THE BEST ENVIRONMENTAL LAWYER IN HOUSTON.

LAVACA BAY
FORMOSA PLASTICS
JIM BLACKBURN SAYS HE'LL WORK WITH ME, AND HE'LL DO IT "PRO BONO"—FOR NOTHING.
I SURE DO APPRECIATE THAT, BLACKBURN. NOW, WHAT DO WE DO FIRST?
WELL, I SUGGEST YOU FIND OUT WHAT POLLUTION THOSE PLANTS ARE MAKING.
BLACKBURN, I CALLED ALL FIVE PLANTS. THEY DON'T TALK TO ME, OR THEY SAY IT'S A PACK OF LIES!
THEY SAY IF I WANT TO KNOW ANYTHING ABOUT THEIR SO-CALLED TOXINS
I HAVE TO GET IT FROM THE EPA !*
* ENVIRONMENTAL PROTECTION AGENCY.
BLACKBURN TELLS ME TO CALL A MEETING SO WE CAN TALK ABOUT THIS WITH THE WHOLE TOWN, MAYBE FIND OUT MORE ABOUT WHAT'S GOING ON.
MATAGORDA BAY
SEADRIFT
ESPÍRITU SANTO BAY

LIMESTONE

SALT

SANDSTONE

The land shaping the bays has formed as layers over millions of years.

75 MILLION YEARS AGO   50 MILLION YEARS AGO

ome mat for known polluter

in controversial plastics firm

...tate, ...ne-ably ...for-...ate." ...De-...tive ...run ...." ...ratic

and Republican legislative leaders agreed to phase out some sales taxes, dedicate state money and support tax abatements, digging deeply into public pockets emptied by years of oil-field recession and real estate busts.

The recipient of this public largesse is Wang, who had to face down an angry crowd of farmers in his homeland as they protested his expansion plans there because of environmental problems.

Texas politicians never mentioned that. Nor that Formosa's Louisiana plant is one of 205 nationwide where the EPA calculated the cancer risk as greatest: 1 in 100.

Nor did they say Formosa's other choice was a southern Louisiana parish where air already was too polluted — partly from Formosa's current discharge — for the plant to expand.

"Your article ought to say: Interested in polluting? Can't do it in Louisiana? Go to Texas," said Willie Fontenot, an environmental coordinator with the Louisiana attorney general's office.

Also not mentioned was an EPA consultant's report that found reason

See FORMOSA on Page 16A.

A COUPLE OF WEEKS LATER I GET A BOX OF DOCUMENTS FROM THE EPA. THEY TELL AN UGLY STORY: HUNDREDS OF VIOLATIONS AND LEAKS OF POISONS TO LAND, AIR, AND WATER.

NOW PEOPLE ARE SAYING I'M NOT A GOOD CITIZEN. NOBODY WANTS TO BE SEEN AROUND ME . . .

The first human settlers used and changed the top layer only, to fish, farm, and raise cattle.

... BUT IN PRIVATE THEY GIVE ME ALL KINDS OF INFORMATION, PHOTOS, NAMES, DOCUMENTS.

MRS. WILSON, I WORK OUT HERE AT FORMOSA. WE'VE GOT PUDDLES OF ACID RIGHT ON THE GROUND, SOAKIN' DOWN INTO THE DRINKIN' WATER!

DIANE, THIS TWC* REPORT FROM LAST YEAR SAYS FORMOSA WASTEWATER KILLED EVERY FISH IN COX'S CREEK!

*TEXAS WATER COMMISSION

WHEN I GIVE COPIES TO THE EPA, THEY SAY IT'S THE FIRST TIME THEY'VE SEEN THESE REPORTS.

THIS IS CRAZY. I'M NOBODY.

SO HOW COME I KNOW MORE THAN THE EPA KNOWS?

MARCH 1990—WE CALL A PUBLIC MEETING TO GIVE OUT OUR REPORT. ABOUT 300 PEOPLE SHOW UP. THE COUNTY IS SPLIT FOR AND AGAINST FORMOSA. STATE AND FEDERAL GOVERN-MENTS SEND PEOPLE DOWN. ENVIRONMENTAL GROUPS COME. SO DOES NATIONAL TV NEWS. THIS TIME I KNOW EXACTLY WHAT TO SAY.

BASED ON THIS DOCUMENTATION, WE DEMAND A HALT TO CONSTRUCTION AT FORMOSA PLASTICS UNTIL THE EPA CARRIES OUT AN ENVIRONMENTAL IMPACT STUDY!

FORMOSA SUPPORTS CALHOUN COUNTY SUPPORTS FORMOSA

♥ we want FORMOSA PLASTICS here! ♥

no mor toxi

APRIL 5—THE TEXAS WATER COMMISSION FINES FORMOSA $244,700, THE BIGGEST FINE IN STATE HISTORY. BUT WHAT ABOUT FEDERAL LAW? WILL THE EPA DO A REAL ENVIRONMENTAL IMPACT STUDY TO BE SURE IT'S SAFE TO BUILD THE PLANTS HERE, OR WILL THEY DO A SHORT ONE THAT LETS FORMOSA START CONSTRUCTION RIGHT AWAY?

WE GET OUR ANSWER THE VERY NEXT DAY.

APRIL 6—THE EPA LEAKS A DRAFT OF ITS ENVIRONMENTAL STUDY: NO SIGNIFICANT IMPACT.

ETHYLENE DICHLORIDE—A CANCER-CAUSING POISON—70,000 TIMES THE FEDERAL LIMIT; VINYL CHLORIDE—ANOTHER CANCER-CAUSING POISON—10,000 TIMES THE FEDERAL LIMIT, PLUS HUNDREDS OF OTHER LEAKS AND VIOLATIONS, AND THIS IS JUST FROM THEIR OLD PEANUT-SIZED PLANT. SO HOW WILL SEVEN HUGE PLANTS HAVE NO SIGNIFICANT IMPACT?

...al Information

...tion: New Source Modification of National Pol...ant Discharge Elimination System (NPDES) Pe... No.TX0085570

Formosa Plastics Corporation Texas P.O. Box 400 101 Formosa Drive Point Comfort, Texas 77978

Type of Facility: Olefins, caustic/chlorine, ethylene dichloride (EDC), polypropylene (PP), high density polyethylene (HDPE), and ethylene glycol (EG) manufacturing.

...cation: In eastern Calhoun County at the Calhoun-Jackson County line near the SH35/FM 1593 juncture east of Lavaca Bay.

...ing: No Significant Impact

...d by: Hector D. Pena, Environmental Scientist Federal Activities Branch, Environmental Services Division, Region 6

Description:

...tion: Formosa Plastics Corporation Texas proposes to ...even (7) plants within its 1,667-acre complex located in ...ed rural areas of Calhoun and Jackson counties near the ...f Point Comfort and Port Lavaca. The proposed expansion ...ated utility plant will be constructed on a 600-acre site ...it to and north of Formosa's existing vinyl chloride ...lyvinyl chloride (VCM/PVC) facility. The Alcoa alumina ...facility is located southwest of the Formosa site.

...e plant will produce 1.5 billion pounds per year (ppy) of ...propylene utilizing eight (8) M.W. Kellogg Millisecond ...naces to crack the propane, butane, or an ethane/propane ...edstock. The caustic/chlorine plant will use the ion exchange ...rocess to produce 1,244 million (MM) ppy of chlorine, 7,406 MM

DRAFT

THE BIGGEST CHEMICAL EXPANSION IN TEXAS, BY A COMPANY WITH A HISTORY OF POLLUTION VIOLATION, DOES NOT REQUIRE AN ENVIRONMENTAL IMPACT STUDY?

I JUST DON'T GET IT. I DON'T KNOW WHAT'S IN THOSE FOLKS' HEADS, BUT IT SURE AIN'T FACTS AND REASON!

NOW, WHAT DOES SOMEBODY WITH NO CLOUT OR MONEY DO TO STOP THE DESTRUCTION OF THESE BAYS?

Later settlers used deeper and deeper layers to mine oil, gas, and water and to store oil and wastes.

WELL, I MIGHT BE A NOBODY, BUT I'M ALL I'VE GOT. SO I DO WHAT I ALWAYS DO WHEN I'M STUCK—I READ. GOTTA START SOMEWHERE.

"AT SOME POINT WE MUST DRAW A LINE ACROSS THE GROUND OF OUR HOME AND OUR BEING . . . AND SAY TO THE BULLDOZERS, EARTHMOVERS, AND CORPORATIONS, 'THIS FAR AND NO FURTHER.'"

—EDWARD ABBEY

"ANYONE COULD DO WHAT I HAVE DONE, GIVEN THE COMMITMENT AND THE DEDICATION."

—GANDHI

"IF I REPENT OF ANYTHING IT IS LIKELY TO BE MY GOOD BEHAVIOR."

—THOREAU

THEN IT GETS REAL CLEAR—

AND REAL SCARY.

UNTIL THE EPA AGREES TO DO A REAL STUDY

. . . I'LL GO ON A HUNGER STRIKE!

RIGHT. HONEST, OPEN, AND NONVIOLENT.

Chemical plants were built on
the bays and changed them in many ways.
The plants use millions of gallons of clean water
daily, to cool their pipes and flush out wastes.

18

The products of petrochemical plants form the basis of our modern life, but the processes often create poisonous wastes and breakdown products. Can we have this life without pollution?

$8.3 million fine proposed for Formosa

By ROBERT CULLICK
Houston Chronicle Austin Bureau

AUSTIN — The Environmental Protection Agency proposed Wednesday a record $8.3 million fine for Formosa Plastics Corp., a company invited by Texas political leaders two years ago to expand its Gulf Coast plant.

"This is the largest proposed administrative penalty in Region 6," said Roger Meacham, spokesman for the Dallas re-

TIME TO CELEBRATE!

BUT NOT FOR US. COUNTY BIGWIGS ARE SO FURIOUS ABOUT THAT FINE, THEY INVITE THE CHAIRMAN OF FORMOSA PLASTICS, Y. C. WANG, TO FLY IN FROM NEW JERSEY FOR A FANCY TIME WITH ALL THE RICH AND FAMOUS DOWN HERE. WANG HEARS I'M GOING TO DEMONSTRATE AT HIS BIG SHINDIG,

SO HE ASKS ME TO MEET WITH HIM BEFOREHAND. WE TALK FOR THREE HOURS.

WHAT IS IT YOU WANT FROM US, MRS. WILSON?

I WANT ONE THING, MR. WANG: ZERO POLLUTION.

Diane, meet Jack Matson. He designs plants that put out ZERO-DISCHARGE.

WHAT? You mean it's possible?

Sure. I've built 'em in Saudi Arabia, Yemen the U.S...

I'M NOT EXACTLY A GUEST AT THE PARTY. I'M IN THE PARKING LOT . . .

The shrimping industry began about the same time as the petro-chemical industry here. Shrimp trawls tear up the bay bottom. More than three quarters of the catch is thrown overboard as "trash fish."

Around the world, fish trawls like this plough up HALF the continental shelf every YEAR!

They're destroying the ecosystem of the sea bottom, and nobody knows the effect this will have!

Australia now allows NO shrimp trawling in the Great Barrier Reef. Shrimpers have to use traps like little lobster traps.

... HANDING OUT FLYERS ABOUT FORMOSA'S HISTORY OF VIOLATIONS IN FRONT OF 200 FORMOSA WORKERS PAID OVERTIME TO PICKET ME. WANG HAS FLOWN IN ABOUT 13 NEWSPAPER REPORTERS FROM TAIWAN SO THEY CAN SEE HOW MUCH TEXANS LOVE HIM AND TAKE THE STORY BACK HOME. IN TAIWAN, HIS NINE PLANTS ARE POLLUTING SO MUCH THAT THOUSANDS OF PEOPLE DEMONSTRATED TO KEEP HIM FROM BUILDING ANY MORE. THAT'S WHY HE HAD TO MOVE OVER HERE!

THE VISITORS READ THE FLYERS.

A FEW WEEKS LATER, I TALK WITH SOME TAIWANESE OFFICIALS AT THEIR HOTEL.

THEN I GET A PHONE CALL.

MRS. WILSON, WE'RE FROM THE TAIWANESE ENVIRONMENTAL UNION.

WE'D LIKE TO INVITE YOU TO TAIWAN TO SEE OUR ENVIRONMENTAL SITUATION.

I LEAVE ON JANUARY 17, THE DAY THE GULF WAR BEGINS.

Shrimp need freshwater to grow into adults.

23

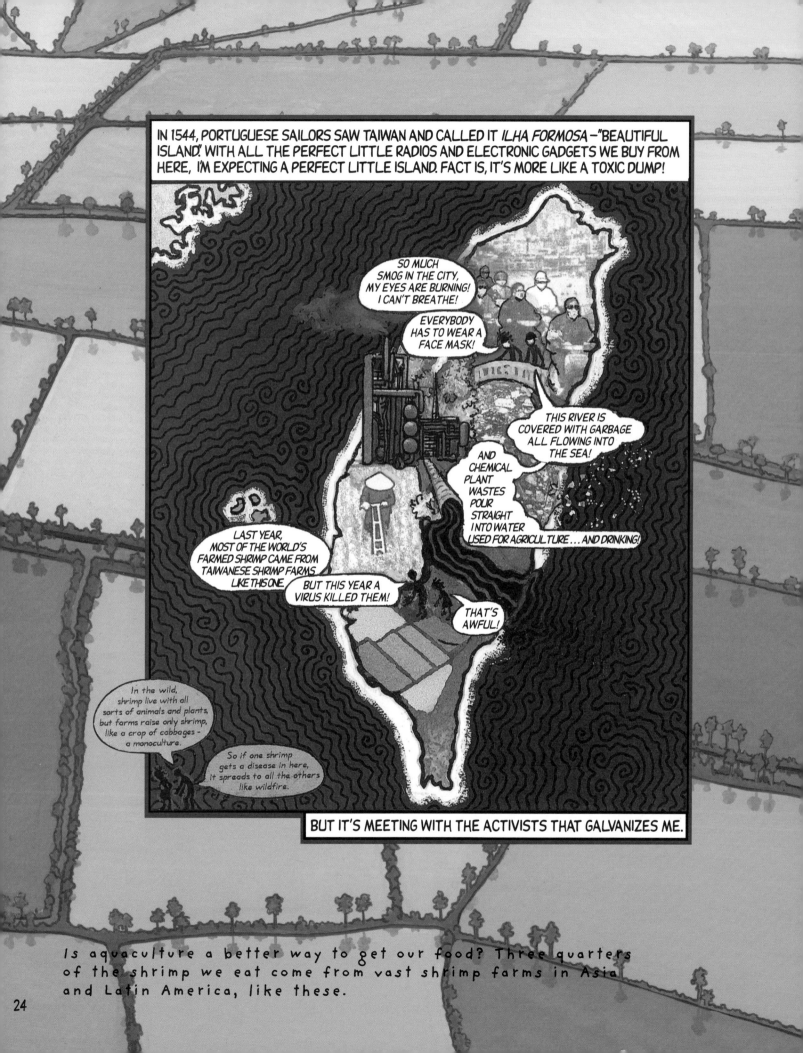

Is aquaculture a better way to get our food? Three quarters of the shrimp we eat come from vast shrimp farms in Asia and Latin America, like these.

Mangrove forests and wetlands protect the land behind them from storms and are nurseries for millions of fish. They are cut down and burned to make shrimp ponds. The ponds are filled with shrimp food, shrimp wastes, lime, pesticides, herbicides, and antibiotics, which all flow into the sea and affect the life there. Eventually, the soil at the bottom of the ponds becomes toxic and the water polluted, and they are abandoned.

WHEN I GET BACK TO SEADRIFT, I GET REAL FOCUSED. THE MINUTE IM NOT SHRIMPING OR WITH THE KIDS, IM WORKING ON FORMOSA—GIVING TALKS, GOING TO MEETINGS AND CONFERENCES, PHONING, FILING SUITS, AND ARGUING FOR ZERO DISCHARGE. IN JULY 1991, A FORMOSA WORKER CALLS ME:

TWO ROADS ARE SHUT DOWN BY A CLOUD OF HYDROCHLORIC ACID. I CALL THE PAPERS AND OSHA.* TWO DAYS LATER, FORMOSA REPORTS THE INCIDENT. THEIR SLOW RESPONSE CAUSES OSHA TO INVESTIGATE. IN SIX MONTHS I LEARN THE RESULTS: $330,000 IN FINES FOR SAFETY AND

HEALTH VIOLATIONS. BUT SHRIMPING IS REAL BAD, AND 12 PERCENT OF CALHOUN COUNTY IS OUT OF WORK. PEOPLE ARE HURTING. SO, THE MORE I FIGHT FOR ZERO POLLUTION, THE MORE FOLKS TURN AGAINST ME. I'M REAL THANKFUL BLACKBURN IS WITH ME, OR I'D BE COMPLETELY ALONE.

*OCCUPATIONAL SAFETY AND HEALTH ADMINISTRATION

Agriculture uses most of the groundwater along the Texas coast, and sometimes much of the river water. In times of drought, farms need still more fresh river water.

ONE EARLY MORNING JUST AFTER I PUT OUT THE NET, A SQUALL HITS.

DESPITE THE RULING THAT THEY HAVE TO DO A THOROUGH ENVIRONMENTAL STUDY FIRST, FORMOSA STARTS BUILDING THE NEW PLANTS. FOR TWO YEARS I WRITE LETTERS, TALK TO POLITICIANS, DEMONSTRATE, GO ON HUNGER STRIKES. NOTHING I DO STOPS CONSTRUCTION.

IN NOVEMBER 1992, I GET A CALL FROM BLACKBURN.

HEY THERE, BLACKBURN! IT DON'T MAKE SENSE, DOES IT? THE FEDERAL GOVERNMENT RULES THAT FORMOSA CAN'T BUILD A THING TILL THE EPA DOES A REAL THOROUGH ENVIRONMENTAL IMPACT STUDY...

...BUT THEY JUST GO AHEAD AND BUILD ALL SEVEN PLANTS!

IT'S AGAINST THE LAW, THEY DON'T HAVE PERMITS, AND NOBODY'S STOPPIN' 'EM!

HUH? OH, I'M FINE. SOMEBODY FLEW OVER IN A HELICOPTER AND SHOT MY DOG. I GOT MY WINDOWS SHOT OUT, MY BOAT ALMOST SUNK AGAIN. HOW HIGH ARE THE CROCODILES ON YOU?

YOU'RE GOIN' TO WHAT? OH, NO, BLACKBURN. YOU'RE NOT GOIN' TO JOIN FORMOSA?

WILSON, I'M NOT JOINING THEM! FORMOSA HAS AGREED TO A STRICT POLLUTION CONTROL PROGRAM.

FOUR PEOPLE ARE GOING TO OVERSEE IT. I'M ONE OF THE FOUR. BUT...

The population of San Antonio will double in 30 years. If citizens use more water from the aquifers under the city, the aquifers will dry up. The city wants to dam part of the river to get fresh water.

WORD GETS OUT FAST THAT I'VE SPLIT WITH BLACKBURN.

TOWNSPEOPLE AND MOST OF MY FAMILY ALREADY HATE MY ACTIVISM, BUT WHEN THEY HEAR I'M NOT SIGNING, THEY BLAST ME. I GO OUT SHRIMPING—OUT TO SUN, WIND, WATER.

YOU'RE TRYIN' TO DESTROY THIS COUNTY!

DIANE, YOU NEED SERIOUS COUNSELING!

YOU'RE NOT THE SAME WOMAN I MARRIED. I DON'T KNOW YOU OR LIKE YOU ANYMORE!

WHEN I COME BACK IN, I'M AS QUIET AS THE BAY.

BLACKBURN'S BEEN AT FORMOSA ALL DAY AND STOPS BY. I GET HIM A CHAIR. WE SIT ON THE EVENING SIDE OF THE DOCK, TALKING ABOUT HOW WE MAKE CHOICES . . .

I WORK FROM MY GUT, BLACKBURN. THIS FEELS WRONG.

WILSON, GOOD CONTRACTS CAN BRING ABOUT POSITIVE CHANGE. YOU'RE TOO STUBBORN AND EMOTIONAL.

. . . UNTIL THE SUN GOES DOWN AND HE DRIVES THE 150 MILES BACK TO HOUSTON.

AM I JUST TOO STUBBORN? NEXT MORNING BEFORE I GO SHRIMPING, I CALL BLACKBURN.

BLACKBURN, I WANT TO SIGN THAT AGREEMENT WITH YOU!

YOU'LL BE KILLING THE BAYS!

WHEN THE ENVIRONMENTALISTS HEAR I'M SIGNING, THEY RIP INTO ME.

TRAITOR!

AS SOON AS I SAY THE WORDS, A HOLE OPENS UP IN ME.

SELLOUT!

BETTER YOU'D DIED ON A HUNGER STRIKE!

MY HEART HAS DROPPED RIGHT OUT. I ONLY WANT TO SLEEP. . . .

Everybody wants more clean, fresh water!

32

NEXT DAY—TIME TO LEAVE FOR THE SIGNING. I CAN'T MOVE. TIME FOR THE SIGNING GOES BY, AND I AM STANDING IN THE SHRIMP HOUSE, CRYING.

MOMMA, YOU SAID YOU'D TAKE US TO THE MALL!

I DRIVE THE 35 MILES HOME FROM THE MALL, LEAVE THE KIDS WITH MY HUSBAND.

I TAKE THE BOAT OUT, NO DEPTH METER, NO LIGHTS.

WHEN I GET BACK HOME, I SLEEP FOR DAYS. THEN I UNPLUG THE PHONE AND SIT ON THE BACK PORCH, DRINKING COFFEE AND WATCHING THE CRANES FLY OVER.

As the river water is used up, the bays will become saltier.
Everything that needs a sweeter mix of water will die—the
shrimp, the whooping cranes, and many, many others.

JANUARY 1994—FORMOSA'S NEW PLANTS HAVE ALL BEEN BUILT, EXCEPT FOR ONE THING:

THEY HAVE LAID A PIPE TO DUMP 15 MILLION GALLONS OF WASTEWATER A DAY INTO SOME OF THE MOST FRAGILE AND LIFE-GIVING AREAS OF THE WHOLE BAY SYSTEM. FORMOSA'S GOT MOST PEOPLE BELIEVING THE DISCHARGE'LL BE HARMLESS. I KNOW IT WON'T BE. AND OF COURSE, THEY DON'T HAVE THE PERMIT FOR THAT WASTEWATER.

I GUESS BLACKBURN'S TAUGHT ME A THING OR TWO OVER ALL THESE YEARS.

BY MYSELF,
I FILE A SUIT
AGAINST
FORMOSA PLASTICS
FOR
DISCHARGING
WITHOUT A PERMIT.

BY MYSELF,
I FILE A SUIT
AGAINST THE EPA
FOR
LETTING FORMOSA
DISCHARGE
WITHOUT A PERMIT.

What's in that wastewater?

NOW, small amounts of poisons, but mostly salt.

SALT!!! What's wrong with salt?

Haven't you read any of the borders in this book?

NOW, MOST FOLKS DON'T CARE ABOUT THIS PIPE—OR THE PERMIT. BUT SHRIMPERS DO. I TALK WITH EVERY LOCAL SHRIMPER I CAN FIND. THEN I GO TO THE VIETNAMESE COMMUNITY. THEY CAME TO SEADRIFT IN THE 70'S AS WAR REFUGEES AND FISHED UP EVERY BLUE CRAB THEY COULD TRAP. BAD COMMUNICATION WITH LOCAL FISHERMEN. REAL UGLY CONSEQUENCES. BAD FEELINGS STILL TODAY. THEY HAVE NO NOTEWORTHY REASON TO BACK ME UP, EXCEPT A BALANCED ASSESSMENT OF THE FACTS. THEY ALSO ALLOW AS HOW SOMETIMES YOU NEED AN EXTRAVAGANT GESTURE TO GRAB FOLKS' ATTENTION.

How can we share this vital water wisely? How can we ALL use less water and keep it clean?

SO 90 LOCAL SHRIMPERS, ANGLO AND VIETNAMESE ALIKE, AGREE TO BLOCK THE SHIP CHANNEL WITH THEIR BOATS. I WILL SINK MY BOAT, THE *SEABEE*, ONTO THE PIPE. ONLY THE *SEABEE'S* MAST WILL REMAIN ABOVE WATER...

...A MONUMENT TO GREED AND TO THE DEATH OF A BAY.

THE DATE IS SET. I GIVE AWAY *SEABEE'S* MOTOR AND CLAMP THE WRENCH ONTO THE PROPELLER SHAFT. ONE TWIST WILL LET THE WATER IN.

NEXT DAY A NORTHER IS WHIPPING ACROSS THE BAY. ONLY SEVEN BOATS SHOW UP FOR THE BLOCKADE.

BUT THE PRESS SHOWS. THE STORY IS TOLD.

AND WASTEWATER CONTINUES TO FLOW OUT OF THAT PIPE.

THE NEXT COUPLE OF WEEKS I LIVE AT THE DOCK ON MY CONFISCATED BOAT.
I'VE STILL GOT MY TWO SUITS IN FEDERAL COURT, AND FORMOSA KNOWS I MIGHT WIN
THEM. SO THEY GET BLACKBURN TO WORK OUT AN AGREEMENT WITH ME.

Mr. Blackburn, those zero-discharge plants are in desert countries – where every drop of water is precious!

And soon, fresh water's going to be that precious here. Folks just don't know it yet.

But you do.

To get zero discharge requires many different systems, some of which are very expensive. How do we decide when freshwater is worth the cost?

28% SALTWATER

SO I AGREE TO DROP MY SUITS AGAINST FORMOSA PLASTICS AND THE EPA, WHILE FORMOSA AGREES TO DO A FEASIBILITY STUDY OF ZERO DISCHARGE AND TO INSTALL ALL PROCESSES ACCEPTED BY A COMMITTEE OF FOUR, WHICH INCLUDES ME. TWO WEEKS LATER, ALCOA SIGNS A SIMILAR AGREEMENT.

MAYBE IT'S TIME TO TURN MORE ATTENTION ON BRITISH PETROLEUM, DUPONT, AND UNION CARBIDE NOW.

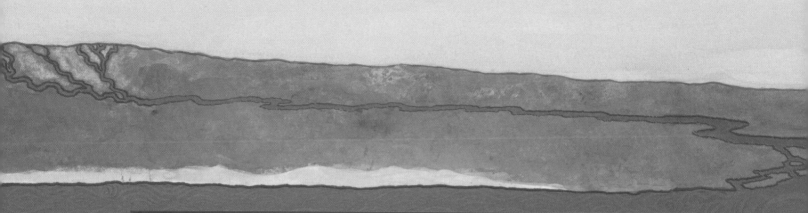

June 2, 2005—An Update on the Story

Plastics still make our modern way of life possible. But now they have leaked into every part of Earth's life system and have been found to be toxic in several ways: Ethylene dichloride and vinyl chloride monomers, the components of PVC, cause neurological disorders. PVC gives off toxic fumes when new and as it breaks down. When it burns (as in incinerators) it gives off poisonous hydrochloric fumes and dioxins. Dioxins are among the most lethal carcinogens and most effective hormone disrupters. Phthalates, used to soften plastics, are hormone disrupters causing genital disorders in male babies. Many countries—*not* including the United States—are phasing out the use of phthalates and working on safe alternatives.

Yet Formosa Plastics is still one of the world's largest PVC producers. A privately held conglomerate, it is so large that it has divided itself into many sub-companies, which are increasingly located in mainland China where disposal of toxic waste is almost completely unregulated.

In 1997, Wilson and Blackburn signed an extensive sustainable development agreement with Formosa that set zero-pollution limits for its land, air, and water discharges and gave workers a part in maintaining safe working conditions. In 1999, after questions were raised about Formosa's new pollution data, and after attempts to form a union were met with harsh resistance by Formosa management, Wilson called their agreements with the company "a hoax on the people, the workers, and the environment," and both she and Blackburn withdrew. The federal government and FBI started a criminal investigation on Formosa's waste stream, and the investigation continues to this day.

In accordance with the zero-discharge agreement, Alcoa Aluminum has installed a

$3 million system that reduces its pollution to zero. It successfully petitioned the EPA to remove aluminum oxide—the pollution that began this whole story—from its list of toxic substances. No one has figured out how to clean up the pool of mercury on the bottom of Lavaca Bay.

Union Carbide also continues to expand. In 2004, Diane was pulled from a tower at Carbide's plant and arrested for staging a sit-in against the corporation's treatment of the survivors of its plant explosion in Bhopal, India. The Bhopal spill is the largest industrial accident in history; thousands were killed and up to 500,000 blinded, their lungs and breathing passageways destroyed by poisonous cyanide gases.

Dupont plans to change its disposal technique in Calhoun County from deep injection wells to a surface waste stream that will enter the Guadalupe River and the bays. The Union Carbide and British Petroleum plants continue to expand. British Petroleum, which owns both Amoco and Atlantic Richfield, now also controls Solarex, making it the world's largest solar power company.

The latest Toxic Release Inventory report states that 4.3 billion pounds of toxic chemicals from the United States were released into the environment in 2002. A thousand times this, or six trillion pounds of chemicals, are produced in our country every year. It is not known how many pounds are toxic, nor which chemicals are released.

Jim Blackburn continues to work as an environmental lawyer and teacher. Diane Wilson sold her commercial shrimping license and now works full time for zero discharge and workers' rights. A large part of their effort is concentrated on supporting workers' rights to create and maintain a healthy environment for themselves at work, at home, and all around the bays.

Hey, Diane!
Did you know that almost HALF of the permanent cropland in Latin America is used for growing coffee?
Look, I NEED my coffee.
Need?